LIVE

Experience Christ's Life

Joel Comiskey

Published by CCS Publishing

www.joelcomiskeygroup.com

Published by CCS Publishing
23890 Brittlebush Circle
Moreno Valley, CA 92557 USA
1-888-344-CELL

Third printing, June 2008

Cover design by Josh Talbot
Editing by Scott Boren

CCS Publishing is the book-publishing division of Joel Comiskey Group, a resource and coaching ministry dedicated to equipping leaders for cell-based ministry.
Find us on the World Wide Web at **www.joelcomiskeygroup.com**

Publisher's Cataloging-in-Publication
(Provided by Quality Books, Inc.)

Comiskey, Joel, 1956-
Live: experience Christ's freedom / by Joel Comiskey.
p. cm.
Includes bibliographical references and index.
ISBN 0975581910

1. Spiritual life--Christianity. 2. Spiritual formation. I. Title.

BV4501.3.C6555 2007 248.4
QBI06-600329

Table of Contents

Introduction. 5

Lesson 1: Finding God. 7

Lesson 2: Establishing a Strong Foundation. 17

Lesson 3: Getting to Know God. 27

Lesson 4: Life with Other Jesus Followers. 35

Lesson 5: Living in Victory. 43

Lesson 6: Triumphing Over the Forces of Evil. 53

Lesson 7: My Life and My Wallet. 63

Lesson 8: Baptism and the Lord's Supper. 71

Appendix: How to Coach Someone using this Material. . . . 79

Index. 83

Introduction

Calling out to Jesus in my bedroom in September 1973 was the smartest thing I've ever done. But in reality, it wasn't my "smarts" that led me to that point. God lovingly drew me to Himself and stirred me to accept His son Jesus. My life since 1973 has been an exciting journey, including the times when my faith has been tested.

You're also in for a wonderful adventure as you read the pages of this book. You'll get to know the heavenly Father who loves you very much. You'll discover what Jesus Christ did for you on the cross and how the Holy Spirit desires to lead and guide your life. You'll learn how to talk to God, read the Bible, and put aside the sins that hinder your relationship with God.

If you're working through this book alone, you would benefit from working with a coach who can help you, answer your questions, and hold you accountable. In the appendix, you'll find tips for coaches.

Additional Resources

Live is part of a five-book series that prepares someone to become a mature follower of Jesus Christ. If you are interested in the other four books that follow in this series, you may purchase them at **www.joelcomiskeygroup.com** or by calling 1-888-344-CELL.

You can use this book individually, in a small group setting, or in a classroom.

Many churches will teach this material in a group setting. This is the normal way to use the material, but it's not the only way. Teaching outlines and PowerPoints for all five equipping books in this series are on CD. Purchase this CD at the CCS web site or by calling the toll free number above.

Finding God

While visiting Athens, Greece, I stayed in a hotel that offered a dazzling view of the Acropolis, where the Parthenon stood. Although just a skeleton today, the Parthenon was once a beautifully ornate temple when the apostle Paul visited Athens during the first century.

At that time, not long after Christ's death and resurrection, Greece was famous for learning and knowledge. Greeks were also known for their worship of many gods. When Paul stood on Mars Hill right outside the Parthenon, he said, "Men of Athens! I see that in every way you are very religious. For as I walked around and looked carefully at your objects of worship, I even found an altar with this inscription: TO AN UNKNOWN GOD. Now what you worship as something unknown I am going to proclaim to you" (Acts 17:22–23).

Like the Greeks, most humans have a religious bent. Within each of us is a longing to find out whether God exists and if He does, then how to know Him.

The Bible declares that God has revealed Himself to people like you and me. He's even provided a way for us to have a personal relationship with Him. To begin that relationship, we have to know where we currently stand and the next step to take.

We need help

The Titanic was touted as the greatest ship of all time. When it first left English shores on its voyage to North America in 1912, everyone thought it was unsinkable. Yet, on April 14, 1912 the ship met an insurmountable obstacle. It crashed into an iceberg that ripped its hull, allowing water to sink it. The ship builders were so confident that they only provided half of the necessary lifeboats. As the ship began to sink, the unfortunate passengers desperately tried to save themselves by jumping onto anything that would float. Most drowned.

We too are passengers on a ship whose destination is eternity. The ship is sinking and our only hope to escape (salvation) is Jesus Christ. Jesus said, "I am the way, the truth, and the life, no one comes to the Father except through me" (John 14:6).

Many people feel that their good deeds or lifestyle is enough to guarantee their eternal security. But the Bible declares, "For all have sinned and fall short of the glory of God (Romans 3:23). The word sin in Romans 3:23 means "to miss the mark." Everyone has missed the mark of God's perfection in thought and action. No one can say he or she is without sin.

A little girl was once watching a sheep eat grass and thought how white it looked against the green background. But when it began to snow she thought, "That sheep now looks dirty against the white snow!" It was the same sheep, but with a different background. When we compare our lives with other people, we may look pretty good, but when we're compared to God's holiness, we realize how far we've fallen short. God's holiness is the standard by which humanity will be judged.

And sin has its consequences. Romans 6:23, says, "For the wages of sin is death, but the gift of God is eternal life in Christ Jesus our Lord." Wages are a reward or recompense for something. The Bible says that the result of sin is death. Spiritual death is the separation of a person from God during life on earth, while physical death is separation from the body. But there's also eternal death. A person, who dies in sin, without receiving the gift of eternal life, is eternally separated from God and goes to a place called hell. This is the ultimate wage of sin.

The good news is that salvation is available for everyone. God sent Jesus to cleanse us from our sin and to restore our broken relationship with God. He wants us to avoid hell, so He has provided a way to bring us back to Himself. Jesus is that way. Jesus offers us the gift of eternal life.

Try IT!

1 Peter 2:24 says, "He himself bore our sins in his body on the tree, so that we might die to sins and live for righteousness; by his wounds you have been healed."

What did Jesus do with our sins?

____

____

How does it make you feel that Christ took your sins upon himself so that you might have a new life?

____

____

____

____

____

____

____

____

Try IT!

Revelation 20:15 says, "If anyone's name was not found written in the book of life, he was thrown into the lake of fire."

What will happen to those whose names are written in the book of life?

____

____

____

And to those who names are not written? ________________

____

____

____

Jesus Christ will show you how to find God

Christmas time comes once a year. Lights go up, gifts are exchanged, and everyone has a good time. But the true meaning of Christmas is often hidden among the presents, buried under our busy schedules, or completely missed as we rush by. The world has shifted its focus from the Savior to the symbols of Christmas. The true meaning of Christmas is Jesus.

The Bible tells us that Jesus was born to give hope to a dark, dying world. My favorite Christmas carol is

> O little town of Bethlehem, how still we see thee lie! Above thy deep and dreamless sleep the silent stars go by. Yet in thy dark streets shineth the everlasting Light; The hopes and fears of all the years are met in thee tonight.

Jesus, the hope of the world, was born in a humble manger on Christmas. God's purpose for this baby boy is best expressed in the often quoted verse from the book of John: "For God so loved the world that he gave his one and only Son, that whoever believes in him shall not perish but have eternal life" (John 3:16).

The ultimate purpose of Christ's birth was His death. Jesus Christ came into this world to die on the cross for our sins. When Christ died on the cross, He took our sins on Himself so that we could experience forgiveness. Billy Graham once said, "God proved his love on the cross. When Christ hung and bled and died, it was God saying to the world, 'I love you.'"

Jesus not only came to take away our sins but also to restore us to a new relationship with the Father. The good news is that through Christ's death on the cross we can have an intimate relationship with a heavenly Father who loves us and has a perfect plan for our lives.

And Jesus didn't stay in the tomb! He rose again. He is alive right now to listen to you and me. The gospel message is summed up in 1 Corinthians 15:3: "that Christ died for our sins according to the Scriptures, that he was buried, that he was raised on the third day."

When I was in sixth grade, I attended a church that didn't speak much about the Bible. I regularly attended Sunday services, but the language was so symbolic that I rarely understood it.

One of my Sunday school teachers, however, loved Jesus and clearly explained that Jesus Christ was alive today and wanted to have a relationship with us. I marveled at his words, thinking that religion was simply a set of symbols about something that happened in the past. Other matters quickly occupied my young mind and I forgot about what my sixth grade teacher taught. Yet, seven years later when I personally received Jesus into my heart at the age of seventeen, this risen, loving Savior named Jesus Christ became my best friend who I talk to continually. My teacher was right. Jesus is alive and well!

Jesus wants to communicate with you. When you talk to Him, He'll hear and answer you. Jesus wants to give you a full and satisfying life on this earth and then eternal life in heaven. The good news of the gospel is that if you believe in Jesus you will receive complete forgiveness of your sin.

God wants a relationship with you

Two cows were grazing alongside a highway when a tanker truck of milk on its way to the distributor happened to pass by. On one side of the truck in big red letters was a sign that read, "Pasteurized, homogenized, standardized, Vitamin A added." One cow turned to the other and remarked, "Makes you feel sort of inadequate, doesn't it?"

Have you ever felt inadequate? Like you just don't measure up? Trying to approach God with good works always leaves us feeling inadequate. The gulf between God and us is great. God is holy and we are not. Jesus Christ, however, has bridged that gap. He has provided the free gift of eternal life. The word gift and the word grace in the Bible both come from the same root word. Both of these words refer to receiving something wonderful we don't deserve.

The relationship that God wants to have with us is based on God's gracious gift. Ephesians 2:8–9 says, "For it is by grace you have been saved, through faith—and this not from yourselves, it is the gift of God—not by works, so that no one can boast." Romans 6:23b says, "the gift of God is eternal life in Christ Jesus our Lord." God loves you and wants to restore you to a right relationship with Himself.

Try IT!

Mark the boxes true or false:

- ☐ Salvation comes as a result of being religious and having good works.
- ☐ Salvation is received only by the grace of God through faith in Jesus Christ.
- ☐ If a person places his or her faith in Jesus alone for salvation, that person can be assured of eternal life.

Then what do we need to do to be saved? Our part is to believe in Jesus and receive the gift of eternal life. What you need to do is believe in Jesus and confess Him as your Lord. Romans 10:9–10 says, "That if you confess with your mouth, 'Jesus is Lord,' and believe in your heart that God raised him from the dead, you will be saved. For it is with your heart that you believe and are justified, and it is with your mouth that you confess and are saved." Someone has said that being "justified" is like being "just as if" I'd never sinned.

The Bible says that those who believe in Jesus will be accepted by God, just as they are, even if they don't deserve it, and with no questions asked. It means that we don't have to deserve such care; it is simply there for us. The grace of God is offered to us as a gift. It is an expression of God's love for us and His unconditional acceptance.

Try IT!

Reread Romans 10:9–10.
Write out what a person needs to do to be saved:

1. ____

2. ____

Do IT!

To become a Christian, ask Jesus to come into your life and make possible a relationship with God. I encourage you say a prayer similar to the one below:

"Lord Jesus, today, I realize that I am a sinner and need your forgiveness. I believe You died on the cross for my sins. I believe You rose again and are alive today. I ask You to forgive my sins and give me the free gift of eternal life. I want to spend the rest of my life learning about you and living for you. I ask for your Holy Spirit to live inside me. Thank You for all You've done for me."

If you have placed your faith in Christ, you can believe that He has forgiven you and has given you a new relationship with God. John 1:12 says, "Yet to all who received him, to those who believed in his name, he gave the right to become children of God." Based on what the Bible says, are you sure of your salvation?

☐ Yes ☐ No

A relationship with Jesus takes a lifetime of getting to know each other. It's not a ritual you perform. Nor is the prayer you prayed the goal; rather it's the place where you begin.

Memorize IT!

Acts 16:31: "Believe in the Lord Jesus, and you will be saved."

The Holy Spirit will help you understand

Human beings didn't plan Christ's death and resurrection. God did. And to make sure we understood it correctly, He gave us His Holy Spirit to enlighten our minds and help us apply God's words.

Jesus says, "But the Counselor, the Holy Spirit, whom the Father will send in my name, will teach you all things and will remind you of everything I have said to you" (John 14:26). The Holy Spirit will help you understand the gospel message and help you live as a Christ-follower. The Spirit will make the Bible clear to you and teach you how to pray.

The Holy Spirit will begin to work in you to produce the good works that God wants to see in your life. Those good works are the result of God working in your life. You're not doing them to receive eternal life; rather, good works are the natural result of someone who is filled with the Holy Spirit and living their lives to please God.

Remember IT!

What stood out to you in this lesson?____________________

____

____

____

____

Main points:

1. The gospel message is clear and simple: Jesus died for our sins, rose again, and offers eternal life to all those who trust in Him alone for their salvation.
2. The Holy Spirit makes the gospel message clear and understandable to us.

Apply IT!

1. Keep growing. You're on a journey all the way to heaven.
2. To keep on the right path there are several things you should do:

   - Start reading the book of John in the New Testament.
   - Fellowship with others. Being part of a small group of Christ-followers will help you understand what it means to be a true believer, and encourage you to grow and to mature spiritually.
   - Finish each session in this book. Look up the Scripture verses and write out your answers.
   - Let someone else know that you've received Jesus in your life. Don't keep the good news to yourself!

Establishing a Strong Foundation

Not long after the Twin Tower "9-11" tragedy, architects started drawing up plans for a new World Trade Center. When I visited the site five years after 9-11, I noticed that construction workers were still working on the foundation of the new structure. They had not yet begun construction on the actual buildings. The foundation was so critical to the new structure; it took years to complete. The workers did finally start building the new World Trade Center—only after the foundation was laid.

Jesus, the master builder, told His disciples how to build a sturdy foundation. The key, according to Jesus, was building the foundation on bedrock, rather than sand. The bedrock is obedience to God's Words. The sand is human reasoning and logic. Jesus said, "Therefore everyone who hears these words of mine and puts them into practice is like a wise man who built his house on the rock. The rain came down, the streams rose, and the winds blew and beat against that house; yet it did not fall, because it had its foundation on the rock. But everyone who hears these words of mine and does not put them into practice is like a foolish man who built his house on sand. The rain came down, the streams rose, and the winds blew and beat against that house, and it fell with a great crash" (Matthew 7:24–27)

God's Word will help you grow

From the moment you received Jesus as Savior, the Holy Spirit began to live in you. One of the key roles of the Holy Spirit is to make God's Word, the Bible, understandable to you. When you read God's Word, start by asking the Holy Spirit to give you wisdom to understand and obey the Bible.

The Holy Spirit will place a hunger in your heart for God's Word because it's food for your soul, just as physical food is for the human body. Like babies need solid food to grow strong, you also need to feed on God's Word to grow spiritually. To grow in your faith in Christ, you'll need a steady diet of God's Word.

Try IT!

Matthew 4:4 says, "Jesus answered, "It is written: 'Man does not live on bread alone, but on every word that comes from the mouth of God.'" According to Jesus, what is our source of spiritual food?

____

____

____

____

How can you apply His Words in your own life?

____

____

____

____

____

____

____

____

God inspired the Bible

An inexperienced seminary graduate went to a church in hope of becoming their next pastor. Thinking he'd impress them with his brilliance, he preached on the inspiration of Scripture. He used as many theological terms as he could find that related to the inspiration of the Bible. He mispronounced a few of them, but assumed that no one would know the difference. One older lady in the congregation was obviously confused by the preacher's jargon, and met him at the back door. She scolded, "Young man, I don't care what you say, I still believe in the Bible!"

Inspiration doesn't have to be that complicated. It simply refers to the truthfulness of the Bible. Inspiration means that we can trust God's Word because God guided the writers of the Bible so that what they wrote was exactly what God wanted them to write. 2 Timothy 3:16 says, "All Scripture is God-breathed and is useful for teaching, rebuking, correcting and training in righteousness."

If you want to know God's plan and will for your life, the Bible is the place to go again and again and again. It will instruct you, correct you, and train you throughout your life. And because it's without error and 100% truthful in all that it affirms, you can trust the words written on each page.

Some people pick and choose which books they "think" are inspired (God-breathed). They might reject the thirty-nine books that make-up the Old Testament, but accept the twenty-seven books of the New Testament. The good news, however, is that we don't have to pick and choose. All sixty-six books of the Bible are God-inspired and perfectly trustworthy.

Try IT!

2 Peter 1:20–21 says, "Above all, you must understand that no prophecy of Scripture came about by the prophet's own interpretation. For prophecy never had its origin in the will of man, but men spoke from God as they were carried along by the Holy Spirit."

What do these verses say about the origins of Scripture? ____________

____

____

When you're reading the Bible, do you believe you are reading the very words of God? Why or why not?

____

____

____

____

____

The Bible is an amazing account of HIStory (God's story)

While bumping through an animal park, we watched a herd of zebras gallop by. We were amazed at the similarity and unity of the herd, but the commentator pointed out that each individual zebra is distinct. "No two zebras," he said, "have the exact same stripes. Each one is different." That same uniqueness characterizes each snowflake that falls to the ground. Different. Distinct. Unique.

The Bible is also distinct and full of rich culture. Consider that it was written by at least forty different authors:

- who lived on two major continents: Europe and Asia
- who wrote during a period of 1600 years
- who belonged to a wide range of cultures and political systems
- who wrote expressing a wide range of emotions (joy, discouragement, etc.).

Yet, these same authors didn't contradict themselves. They all wrote about the revelation of God's love through the person of Jesus Christ.

The Bible is the true story of God at work since He created this world and placed Adam and Eve in it. It tells us about the history of God's relationship with His people—from the creation of the world to Jesus and the early church and all the way to what will happen when Jesus comes back again. The Bible is also full of rich teachings about how God wants His children to live.

Even though the Bible was written over a period of 1600 years, it's just as relevant to us today as it was to the original readers.

The Bible is organized into two sections—Old Testament and New Testament. There are 66 books in the Bible (39 in the Old Testament and 27 in the New Testament). If you don't know where to find a book in the Bible, go to the table of contents in front and find the book's page number. You'll notice that each book has chapters and verses (with the exception of Philemon, 2 John and 3 John). If you're asked to turn to find John 3:3, for example, you would go to the book of John, then to chapter three, and then you'd look for verse three.

Do IT!

Read one chapter per day, starting with the book of John in the New Testament. Here are some questions to get started:

1. What did you learn from the chapter?
2. Was there a particular verse that stood out to you?
3. How are you going to practice what you learned in your own life?

Finding the right translation

Most Bible translations attempt to make the Bible relevant to today's culture and language. Good translations faithfully reflect the original biblical languages, which are Hebrew and Aramaic in the Old Testament and Greek in the New Testament.

Some translations try to match the original biblical languages word for word. The New American Standard Bible and the New King James Version are examples of this. Other translations attempt a sentence for sentence equivalence. This gives more clarity and flow and makes it easier to understand. The New International Version and the New Revised Standard Version follow the sentence for sentence structure. Still other translations provide a thought for thought translation that allows even greater adaptation from the original to modern English. The Message Bible, the Contemporary English Version and The New Living Translation all follow the thought for thought format.

Try IT!

Which of the Bible translations above have you previously heard about?

____

____

____

What was one new thing you learned about Bible translations?

____

____

____

____

____

The best translations seek to balance accuracy of the original text with easily understood modern day language. Many people are familiar with the King James Version, but it contains English words used 400 years ago. Many of those words have become meaningless to us today.

I personally recommend the New International Version of the Bible because of its faithfulnesss to the original language and because it's easily understood in modern English. However, if you have questions on what is the best translation (and there are differences of opinion on this subject), speak with the pastor of your local church or the person who is coaching you through this material.

Memorize IT!
Psalm 119:11: "I have hidden your word in my heart that I might not sin against you."

Obeying God's Word

A missionary translator was trying to find a word for obedience in the native language. Obedience was a virtue seldom practiced in that tribe, so the missionary found it very difficult to find the right word. As he returned home from the village one day, he whistled for his dog and it came running at full speed. An old native, seeing this, said admiringly in the native tongue, "Your dog is all ear." Immediately the missionary knew he had his word for obedience.

Actually the Hebrew word for obey means "to hear." To truly hear God's Words implies obedience as opposed to simply receiving information. The Greek phrase for obey means "to hear under." The idea of obedience in the New Testament is a hearing that takes place under the authority or influence of the speaker, thus leading to compliance with what is being taught. James writes, "Do not merely listen to the word, and so deceive yourselves. Do what it says" (1:22).

As you read God's Word each day, He'll show you what He wants you to do. And because the Holy Spirit now lives in you, He'll give you the power to obey God's Word.

The Bible is not a rulebook of do's and don'ts. Jesus said, in Matthew 22:37–40: "'Love the Lord your God with all your heart and with all your soul and with all your mind.' This is the first and greatest commandment. And the second is like it: 'Love your neighbor as yourself.' All the Law and the Prophets hang on these two commandments."

The most important thing we can do is to love God first. We do this by worshipping Him, praying to Him, reading His Word and obeying Him.

The second most important commandment is to love our neighbors. Our neighbor is first and foremost those who are closest to us. If you're married, for example, your spouse should be your first priority. If you're a child, remember to obey and honor your parents first and foremost after Jesus. Someone said, "Success is having those closest to you love and respect you the most."

Beyond those closest to us, God wants us to love and serve those who we don't know—which means sharing the good news about Christ's life, death and resurrection with those who we meet. The last instructions Jesus gave His followers was to share the good news with others. Jesus said, "All authority in heaven and on earth has been given to me. Therefore go and make disciples of all nations, baptizing them in the name of the Father and of the Son and of the Holy Spirit, and teaching them to obey everything I have commanded you" (Matthew 28:18–20).

Christ's last words to his disciples are generally known as the "Great Commission." Our mission from Jesus is to make disciples everywhere. A disciple is a person who obeys, follows, and imitates Jesus Christ.

Try IT!

Tell someone else about what Jesus has done in your life. Don't think you have to know a lot about the Bible before telling others about Jesus. Evangelizing is simply sharing with others what God has done in your life.

Why do people think they have to know so much before they can tell others about Jesus?

Remember IT!

What impacted you most from this lesson?____________________

____

____

____

____

____

____

____

____

____

Main points:

1. God inspired those who wrote God's Word so that all that they wrote is exactly what God wanted them to say. God's Word is without error in its original form.
2. The Bible is an amazing collection of sixty-six books written over a period of 1600 years by many authors who lived in different cultures.

Apply IT!

1. Write out a prayer right now asking God to help you to understand the importance of God's Word.
2. Before reading God's Word, ask God to help you understand it. You might pray a prayer like this, *"Lord, open my spiritual understanding so that when I read Your Word, I might discover Your will for me."*
3. Read one chapter of God's Word each day.

Getting to Know God

Jesus used the Aramaic term Abba when addressing His Father in heaven. Jesus's use of Abba indicates a unique and intimate relationship of deep trust with God. It is not a proper name for a father, but it is a personal name for him. Slaves in ancient times were forbidden to use this form of direct address when speaking to the head of the family. One of the early Christ-followers named Paul used the same word in Romans 8:15: "For you did not receive a spirit that makes you a slave again to fear, but you received the Spirit of sonship. And by him we cry, "Abba, Father."

As a believer in Jesus, you are invited into an intimate relationship with God the Father. He wants to become your Dad. You can now freely use the phrase, Abba, Father. Some religions promote a sovereign deity that is cold, distant, and angry. Christianity speaks of a loving Father. Yes, He's 100% holy and just, but unlike pagan gods, He's caring and personal. He has your best interest in mind.

Jesus calls you His friend. He says, "I no longer call you servants, because a servant does not know his master's business. Instead, I have called you friends, for everything that I learned from my Father I have made known to you" (John 15:15). And this friendship extends to your relationship with God the Father and the Holy Spirit.

You can talk to God as you would talk to your best friend. If you have good news to share or a problem to discuss, go directly to Him. You can talk to Him any time. He wants to hear everything.

As in any relationship, great communication is necessary for the relationship to grow and stay intimate.

Developing a Relationship with God

My dad taught Psychology at Long Beach City College for nearly thirty-five years. As a teacher, his students knew how to contact him, whether by phone or appointment. These students also knew, however, that it was not acceptable to call late at night or knock at my dad's door without a prior appointment. Their access was confined to my dad's office hours at school. Protocol dictated the type of contact between professor and student. This protocol, however, didn't apply to me. I could meet with my dad anytime day or night. Students had some access; I had full access.

You are God's child and have full access. You have the right to come boldly before God day or night. Because you are made in God's image and are born of the Spirit, you are given the privilege of developing an intimate relationship with Him.

Try IT!

Do you find it hard to believe that you have God's complete attention, full access to him?

____

____

____

____

Yet, notice I used the word "develop." Although you have full access, you can choose not to use that access. As you grow as a Christian, you'll realize more and more how important it is to continually approach your heavenly Father for everything.

The more you talk to God, the more He'll reveal who He is to you. You'll become familiar with his still small voice, which is often like an impression that pops into your mind. Such impressions are always peaceful and gentle—as opposed to fearful and doubtful. Just as we know the familiar voice of a mother or father, we can learn to hear the gentle voice of God. As you learn to listen to your heavenly Father, your ability to hear and discern His voice will grow.

Prayer is most effective when you believe that the One you're talking to actually is listening. Without this ingredient, prayer can be a long, drawn-out exercise of trying to appease a God who either isn't there or doesn't want to hear.

Matthew 6:7 says, "And when you pray, do not keep on babbling like pagans, for they think they will be heard because of their many words." Prayer doesn't consist in repeating certain words, but rather prayer should come from the heart. Prayer involves sincerely expressing yourself to God, rather than reciting a prayer formula.

Try IT!

Read Matthew 6:5–6.
What does God tell us to do (as opposed to the Pharisees)?

____

What has been your experience thus far with spending time alone with God?

____

____

Before receiving Jesus Christ as my Savior, I repeated long-drawn out prayers to a God who seemed so cold and distant. I stopped only after I felt I had appeased this deity by my diligent effort. After accepting Jesus and being filled with the Spirit, my prayers became warm, compassionate, intimate talks with God.

Prayer is mainly focused on building your relationship with God. Jesus wants to become your best friend. He wants to spend time with you. You now have confidence to enter into His presence because of the special relationship you have with Him.

I don't like to offer precise prayer formulas to recite because they might quench your creativity and personal relationship with God. Your relationship with God should stay simple and dynamic.

Prayer is not bound by time or place. 1 Thessalonians 5:17 says, "pray continually." You can pray when you wake up in the morning, during the day, or before going to bed. You can pray to God anytime. You can pray while walking down the street, at work, or in a forest.

Give thanks to God

King David had a great relationship with God. Often when David approached God, he began with praise and worship: "Praise be to you, O LORD, God of our father Israel, from everlasting to everlasting. Yours, O LORD, is the greatness and the power and the glory and the majesty and the splendor, for everything in heaven and earth is yours. Yours, O LORD, is the kingdom; you are exalted as head over all. Wealth and honor come from you; you are the ruler of all things. In your hands are strength and power to exalt and give strength to all. Now, our God, we give you thanks, and praise your glorious name" (1 Chronicles 29:10–13).

Prayer is NOT simply asking God for things. It's communion with the King. It's all about a relationship with the One you'll be spending eternity with. I recommend entering God's presence with worship and praise. Thanking Him not only honors Him but also opens our heart to a deeper relationship. Psalm 96:4 says, "For great is the LORD and most worthy of praise; he is to be feared [respected] above all gods."

Do IT!

Take a few moments now and write down some things that God has done for you. Practice giving thanks to God now.

Admit to God your sins and faults

You might have heard the phrase, "there's an elephant in the room." This is a slang expression that means "something is wrong that no one wants to talk about." Many Christians don't pray because there's an elephant in the room. They know they've sinned and they know God knows, so it's best to ignore God—or so they think.

It's pointless, however, to hide sin from God. He knows everything. You can't hide from Him. Don't let sin rob your relationship with God. 1 John 1:9 says, "If we confess our sins, he is faithful and just and will forgive us our sins and purify us from all unrighteousness." God always offers us a way back to Him. He doesn't make it hard. Confess your sin to Him and allow Him to restore you. Proverbs 28:13 says, "He who conceals his sins does not prosper, but whoever confesses and renounces them finds mercy."

Ask Him for whatever you need

God wants and expects us to pray for our own needs. I first heard this poem in Bible school and it's stuck with me ever since: "You are coming to a King, large petitions with you bring. For His power and grace are such, you can never ask too much."

Try IT!

Read Ephesians 3:20.
What does God promise concerning answered prayer?

____

____

What impact would believing this have on the way you pray?

____

____

I've found that God gives us more than we can ask for or imagine. He's always planning something a little bit better than we can ask for or think possible.

Jesus was constantly telling His disciples to ask in His name. God is honored when you ask him to supply your needs. Boldly bring to Him your physical needs (e.g., food, clothing, a job), your emotional needs (e.g., fears, doubts, worries), and your need for spiritual growth in Christ (e.g., power to evangelize, use of spiritual gifts).

Sometimes God will burden your heart to pray for someone. It may be that God wants to work in that person's life through your prayers. One Sunday evening in April 1912, an American woman was very weary, yet could not sleep because of a burden for her husband who was then in mid-Atlantic, homeward bound on the Titanic. She kept on praying until about five o'clock in the morning, when at last a great peace came upon her and she slept.

Meanwhile her husband, Colonel Gracie, was among the hundreds who were frantically trying to launch the lifeboats from the Titanic. He had given up all hope of saving himself, and was doing his best to help the women and children. As the ship plunged into the deep, he was sucked down in the giant whirlpool. Instinctively he began to swim under water, ice cold as it was. Suddenly he came to the surface and found himself near an over-turned life boat. He and several others climbled aboard and were picked up by another lifeboat, about five in the morning, the very time that peace came to his praying wife!

The Bible says, "This is the confidence we have in approaching God: that if we ask anything according to his will, he hears us. And if we know that he hears us—whatever we ask—we know that we have what we asked of him" (1 John 5:14–15).

Try IT!

Mark the below sentences that are true:

- ☐ Prayer means repeating the same words and phrases.
- ☐ We must beg God to give us exactly what we ask for.
- ☐ When praying, we must give thanks to God for everything.
- ☐ God wants us to pray for our own needs and the needs of others.

One of those prayers that God loves to hear is the prayer for non-Christians. He loves it when we enter the battleground and pray fervently for others. You might start praying for certain people on a daily basis.

I first experienced the power of answered prayer after I began to pray daily for my friend Glen in 1979. Glen and I were friends in elementary school and throughout high school. When I was seventeen, I received Jesus but Glen continued in wild living. God helped me to pray for Glen just about every day for ten years, even though I only saw him once or twice in that time period. One day Glen suddenly walked into the church where I was pastoring. That same day he received Jesus and weeks later, I had the privilege of baptizing Glen and his girlfriend Karen. Months later, I performed Glen's wedding to Karen. I saw God answer prayer in a powerful way. The key is to keep on praying until the answer comes.

Memorize IT!
Psalm 66:18, "If I had cherished sin in my heart, the Lord would not have listened."

God responds to ALL prayers

Here are some principles that will help you to know how God answers prayer. God responds to all prayers in at least four ways. He might give you a:

1. Green light. This simply means that what you're asking for is within His will. God has even stirred you to make that request and now He's answering it.
2. Yellow light. God knows it's best not to fulfill immediately what we're asking for. Psalm 40:1 says, "I waited patiently for the LORD; He turned to me and heard my cry." Perhaps God wants to resolve other things in your life before granting that particular request. Be patient.
3. Red light. God might simply say NO. It's not in His will. He knows your request is not best for you or His eternal purpose. Since God knows you much better than you know yourself, His judgment is always right. Also remember that at times God might

need to purify your motivations and values. James 4:3 says, "When you ask, you do not receive, because you ask with wrong motives, that you may spend what you get on your pleasures."

4. U-turn. In this situation, God is asking you to refocus your prayers. Prayer, in fact, often changes us in the process of praying. At times, God will have you pray for something else because He wants to give you something even better than what you're asking for. Our continual prayer must be "May your will be done and not my own." God is sovereign. He knows what is best for us and always answers in our best interest. Jesus says in Matthew 6:8 that the "Father knows what you need before you ask him."

Remember IT!

Which verse of Scripture impressed you most from this lesson? Why?

____

____

____

____

Main points:

1. Prayer at its highest form is getting to know God.
2. Prayer starts with worship and praise and continues with confession and petition (asking).
3. God always answers prayer but He doesn't always say YES.

Apply IT!

1. Write on a sheet of paper friends and family who don't know Jesus Christ as Savior and Lord. Begin to pray daily for them.
2. Reflect on a time when God said no to your prayers. Think of another time when He said yes.

Life with Other Jesus Followers

Several years ago, the nation's news programs were dominated by the story of a young woman from California who worked as a congressional aide and mysteriously disappeared. Over and over again, her physical description was published—height, hair color, eye color, and distinguishing characteristics. By virtue of that detailed description, there was hope that if someone should see her, she could be identified and brought home to her worried family.

Every day we encounter occasions in which we have to identify objects, such as a car in the parking lot or a lost dog. Some things are easier to identify while others are less concrete and more subjective. An example is the church of Jesus Christ. If you were asked to identify the church of Jesus Christ, what would you say? Would you point to a particular building? A denomination? An event on Sunday morning?

What is the church?

The essence of the word church (Greek word=ekklēsia) in the New Testament is an assembly of believers. The writers of the New Testament repeatedly referred to the church as either a group of people in the city or one particular household. When Paul wrote in 1 Corinthians 1:2, "To the church of God in Corinth" he was referring to all believers in the city. Yet at the end of the same book, Paul said, "Aquila and Priscilla greet you warmly in the Lord, and so does the church that meets at their house" (1 Corinthians 16:19). For the first 300 years after Christ's resurrection, the New Testament Church existed as individual house churches. When possible the house churches in a particular city would celebrate together. Yet, the normal church gathering was in the home.

The focus of the church is never on the building but always on the people. Sadly, many today equate church with a building. The true church, however, consists of those who have placed their faith in Jesus Christ and live under His Lordship. The church is a spiritual family of brothers and sisters who have the same Father in heaven. The church is God's vehicle on earth to save, disciple, and prepare workers to continue the process of reaching people.

Try IT!

Read Hebrews 10:24–25.
What are Christians called to do, according to these verses?

____

____

Do you feel the need to meet regularly with other believers? Why or why not?

____

____

____

____

Cell-based local church

The earliest believers in Jerusalem met both in homes and in the Jewish temple. Acts 2:42, 46 says this about the earliest church: "They devoted themselves to the apostles' teaching and to the fellowship, to the breaking of bread and to prayer … Every day they continued to meet together in the temple courts. They broke bread in their homes and ate together with glad and sincere hearts." As long as possible, the early church met together openly to hear the apostle's teaching. Yet, they also met from house to house.

Try IT!

Read Acts 5:42.
Where did the apostles meet according to this verse?

____

____

Why are both large and small meetings beneficial?

____

____

____

The apostle Paul continued to preach and teach publicly and privately. He said to the Ephesian elders, "You know that I have not hesitated to preach anything that would be helpful to you but have taught you publicly and from house to house (Acts 20:20).

Today believers seem to grow best when they meet publicly (normally on Sunday) for the preaching of the Word and weekly in a house group. This approach to church life is commonly called the cell-based church or cell church.

The Cell

While called by different names, the cell group forms the basic building block in the church. The most common definition of a cell and the one followed in this book is: *A group of 3-15 people who meet weekly outside the church building for the purpose of evangelism, community, and discipleship with the goal of multiplication.*

The cell is the church, just as the Sunday worship service is. It simply serves a different purpose. The larger service is to hear teaching and to worship with all those in the local church. The cell is more personal; it's a time to apply God's Word to our daily lives.

Your regular attendance in a cell group will help you grow spiritually. You'll build lasting relationships on your Christian journey. You'll feel the freedom to talk about your struggles and find those who are wrestling with similar issues.

When Jim decided to attend one of the church's cell groups, the hardest part was walking through the door for the first time, but his fears were unfounded. He felt very comfortable, and the group didn't pressure him to talk. The next meeting was easier, and he even made a few friends. Within the first month, after hearing others transparently talk about their own needs, he felt comfortable enough to share personal prayer requests. It's been one year now since Jim joined the cell group. His life has been transformed. His relationship with his wife Cathy has also improved. He gets into his car for work each morning knowing he has a cell community with whom he can share his struggles. He realizes now more than ever that he needs fellow believers as he walks through the Christian life.

God never intends for a Christian to live as an island. He wants each believer to grow with other fellow Christians. Many are accustomed to sitting in church, hearing a great message, but they never move beyond the information stage. The intimate environment of the cell will help you to live the Christian life, not just understand it. The cell is a place where you can taste authentic community. It's the place where you can feel a real sense of belonging.

Try IT!

List several reasons why you will need to meet each week in a cell group:

____

____

____

____

____

We all know that there are many good things that might distract us from attending the cell meeting each week, so it's important from the beginning to make a firm commitment to be present. Scriptures says, "Let us not give up meeting together, as some are in the habit of doing, but let us encourage one another—and all the more as you see the Day approaching" (Hebrews 10:25). You have something to contribute to the ministry of the church; other believers need your contribution.

Typically, one person will serve the group as the leader or facilitator. Someday, in fact, when you have matured, you can also facilitate a cell group and help those in the group to grow spiritually in their relationship with Christ and one another.

Do IT!

Make a commitment to attend the cell each week.

The worship service

In the early church, both cell and celebration were essential because of the practical benefits that both offered. In the celebration, God appointed gifted teachers to feed the entire flock of God. We read in Acts 2:42 that the earliest believers in Jerusalem devoted themselves to the "apostles teaching." How exciting to hear from the very apostles who walked closely with Jesus Christ.

The early Jewish believers needed clear teaching concerning how Jesus, the Messiah, related to the Old Testament. With enemies from within and without ready to pounce on the tender church, those believers needed a firm foundation. The apostles also imparted the vision to reach the entire world during church meetings. After all, the commission of the master was to disciple all nations.

Try IT!

What are the benefits of gathering all the cells together to worship and learn God's Word?

____

____

How are you going to apply this lesson in your own life?

____

____

Cell-based churches have regular celebration services in which all the cells come together for worship and the Word. This is an important time to hear God's Word and worship together. In the celebration, those who are called to preach and teach God's word may do so. It's a time for the leaders to cast vision and direction with everyone present. Many cell-based churches convert the Bible message on Sunday morning into a discussion-based cell guide for use the following week.

Commit yourself to regular attendance at both the cell and celebration meetings so that you receive the full benefit of the cell church.

Memorize IT!

Ephesians 4:11-12: "It was he [God] who gave some to be apostles, some to be prophets, some to be evangelists, and some to be pastors and teachers, to prepare God's people for works of service, so that the body of Christ may be built up."

Benefits of joining one local church

Billy Graham once said, "If you find a perfect church, don't join it; you'd spoil it." The perfect church doesn't exist. That's because the perfect person doesn't exist and churches are made up of imperfect people. Yet, God has chosen to work through imperfect people.

Some people jump from church to church before they get to know anyone intimately. I encourage you to stick with one local church so that you can grow stronger in your relationship with God. Others will have a chance to get to know you and help you grow. God will also use you to help those in the church.

Try IT!

Why is it important to participate in one local church, rather than hopping from church to church?

____

____

____

Our closest friends overlook our imperfections. This holds true for families and churches. You'll need to learn to look past personalities that rub you wrong and people that you disagree with. God will mold and shape you in the process.

God has raised up pastors and teachers to help us grow. When I was a new Christian, a person from a false cult tried to draw me away from Jesus. But on the following Sunday I learned about the dangers of this particular brand of false teaching from my local church pastor. After that teaching, I realized my need for a spiritual mentor. God has raised up pastors and teachers in His Church. Ephesians 4:11–12 says, "It was he [God] who gave some to be apostles, some to be prophets, some to be evangelists, and some to be pastors and teachers, to prepare God's people for works of service, so that the body of Christ may be built up."

Commit to a local church that lives by God's Word and depends on the Holy Spirit. Stick with that church—even if it has warts. All of them do. In this way, you will flourish in your Christian life. Hebrews 13:17 says, "Obey your leaders and submit to their authority. They keep watch over you as men who must give an account. Obey them so that their work will be a joy, not a burden, for that would be of no advantage to you." Welcome the chance to receive spiritual preparation from leaders who know you personally. God has called certain people to serve the local church.

Remember IT!

How did God speak to you through this lesson? ________________

____

____

____

Main points:

1. God wants you to be accountable to one local church.
2. Cell-based churches emphasize both cell and celebration, and you should be part of both a cell and the larger celebration.

Apply IT!

1. Write down in your own words why it's important to be part of a cell group. ________________________________
2. Write down why it's important to be part of a worship service.

   ____

   ____

3. Make an effort to contact a small group leader and actually attend a small group meeting this month.

Lesson Five

Living in Victory

I heard the true story of an impoverished man from Texas who could barely feed his family. He scrambled around to provide their bare necessities. Somehow he managed to place enough food on the table at the end of the day. His only earthly possession was a poor shack that stood on a dusty piece of land he inherited from his parents.

Their situation changed drastically when oil was discovered on his property. He became a multi-millionaire as the result, and his family eventually inherited the treasure.

In one sense, this man was a millionaire even when he could barely feed his family. The oil was always there and it was his all the time. He just didn't know it.

The Bible declares that we are rich (co-heirs) in Christ. Romans 8:17 says, "Now if we are children, then we are heirs—heirs of God and co-heirs with Christ." Part of the Christian journey is to understand what we already possess. Here's just a taste from the first chapter in the book of Ephesians:

- God has blessed us in the heavenly realms with "every spiritual blessing in Christ" (Ephesians 1:3).
- "He lavished on us all wisdom and understanding "(Ephesians 1:8).
- "He made known to us the mystery of his will according to his good pleasure, which he purposed in Christ" (Ephesians 1:9).
- "He predestined us according to the plan of him who works out everything in conformity with the purpose of his will" (Ephesians 1:11).
- We are "marked in him with a seal, the promised Holy Spirit" (Ephesians 1:13).

See yourself as God sees you

Unlike the impoverished man from Texas, many live at ease and have plenty of earthly possessions. Yet, they are driven to achieve a sense of worth or acceptance based on external recognition. Many people become workaholics because they never received love and acceptance at home. Others withdraw and become apathetic as they give up hope of true love and acceptance. This type of outcome-based living can never fulfill a person's emotional needs.

Perhaps you've missed out on that love and acceptance while growing up. The sad truth is that parents often fail.

The good news is that God is now your Father, and He desires to shower His love and grace on you. He wants you to see yourself as He sees you. As you begin to live out the dream that God has for you, your life will overflow with blessing. After reading each verse, boldly repeat what each verse says about you:

- John 1:12 says, "Yet to all who received him [Jesus], to those who believed in his name, he gave the right to become children of God." <u>"I am a child of God."</u>
- Romans 8:31–32 says, "What, then, shall we say in response to this? If God is for us, who can be against us? He who did not spare his own Son, but gave him up for us all—how will he not also, along with him, graciously give us all things? <u>"God is on my side".</u>
- 2 Corinthians 5:17 says, ˝Therefore, if anyone is in Christ, he is a new creation; the old has gone, the new has come! <u>"I'm a new person in Christ."</u>
- Philippians 4:13: "I can do everything through him who gives me strength." <u>"I am in Christ and therefore I can do all things through Him."</u>
- Romans 6:18 says, "You have been set free from sin and have become slaves to righteousness." <u>"I am set free from sin."</u>
- Ephesians 2:10 says: "For we are God's workmanship, created in Christ Jesus to do good works, which God prepared in advance for us to do." <u>"God has a perfect plan for my life."</u>
- Ephesians 3:20 says, "Now to him who is able to do immeasurably more than all we ask or imagine, according to

his power that is at work within us." "God is capable of giving me far more than I could ever ask for."

This is just a taste of the many, many promises God has given us in the Bible. As you begin to live by these promises and repeat them, your life will begin to change. I encourage you to memorize them so that you may repeat them throughout the day.

Try IT!

Make one statement (as I've done above) from each of the following verses:
Romans 8:17 says, "Now if we are children, then we are heirs—heirs of God and co-heirs with Christ."

I am ____

1 Corinthians 6:19 says, "Do you not know that your body is a temple of the Holy Spirit, who is in you, whom you have received from God?"

I am ____

John 15:15 says, "I [Jesus] no longer call you servants, because a servant does not know his master's business. Instead, I have called you friends, for everything that I learned from my Father I have made known to you."

I am ____

Ephesians 1:3–4 says, "Praise be to the God and Father of our Lord Jesus Christ, who has blessed us in the heavenly realms with every spiritual blessing in Christ. For he chose us in him before the creation of the world to be holy and blameless in his sight."

I am ____

Do IT!

Start right now to think the thoughts that God says about you in the Bible. Stop condemning yourself because you don't feel worthy. Believe what God says about you.

Start living in Spiritual Freedom

One intriguing fact of slavery in the U.S. was that the slaves were officially freed on January 1, 1863 when Lincoln signed the Emancipation Proclamation. Those slaves weren't practically freed, however, until General Robert E. Lee surrendered the army of northern Virginia at noon on April 9, 1865. With Lee's surrender, the rest of the confederate forces put down their arms in a matter of weeks. Slaves were finally able to leave their plantations as free persons.

The Bible says that Jesus has paid the price for us to be free. We are free. This declared truth cannot be reversed. Experiencing Christ's freedom, on the other hand, requires something additional. It means dealing with areas of sin and strongholds and allowing Christ to be Lord of every area of our lives.

Unfortunately, many believers are enslaved to thoughts, actions, and sins that keep them from spiritual victory. It's one thing to hear the proclamation that you're set free from sin and slavery. It's quite another thing to live in that freedom. If a person has been incarcerated in a prison for many years, it takes a while to adjust to the new freedoms in the real world. Many who have "accepted Jesus" are not living in freedom because they are enslaved to sinful practices. Jesus said in John 8:34, 36: "I tell you the truth, everyone who sins is a slave to sin. . . . So if the Son sets you free, you will be free indeed."

Memorize IT!

Philippians 4:13: "I can do everything through him who gives me strength."

Try IT!

Read 2 Corinthians 3:17.
What should characterize those who are filled with the Spirit?

___

___

___

Are you experiencing Christ's freedom in your life? Why or why not?

___

___

___

___

___

___

___

___

___

One area in which many believers are bound is unforgiveness. It might be the failure to forgive another person or to forgive ourselves. Jesus wants to set you free from this, and He wants to give you the power and grace to forgive. Matthew 18:21–22 says, "Then Peter came to Jesus and asked, 'Lord, how many times shall I forgive my brother when he sins against me? Up to seven times?' Jesus answered, 'I tell you, not seven times, but seventy-seven times.'"

Try IT!

Read Ephesians 4:32.
Why should we forgive others according to this verse?

____

____

____

____

____

Whom do you need to forgive?

____

____

____

____

____

Forgiveness is a decision and involves our will. It's not enough to forgive once or twice. Forgiveness must become our lifestyle. If you desire to be free in Christ, you must decide to forgive all those who have offended you, independently of your feelings. Colossians 3:13 tells us that we need to forgive "whatever grievances you may have against one another."

Christ forgave us by voluntarily taking upon Himself the consequences of our actions. He then made the conscious decision to not hold us accountable ever again for those actions. We are to forgive in the same manner.

Remember that forgiving others will free you from the bondage of bitterness and resentment.

God is still working on you

God is working on you "24/7" to set you completely free from whatever enslaves you. The story is told of Michelangelo passing by a huge chunk of marble that lay by the roadside. Another sculptor had become discouraged with the marble and discarded it. Michelangelo began to stare at that chunk of marble. He continued to stare until one of his friends became impatient and said, "What are you staring at?" Michelangelo looked up and said, "I'm staring at an angel." He could see something wonderful and worthwhile in a broken piece of stone. God sees something wonderful in you, and He's already started the process of transformation. He will continue this process until He takes you to heaven to be with Him. The good news is that along the way He is molding and shaping you into His image.

Becoming spiritually mature is a process that lasts a lifetime. You will have spurts of growth from time to time, but you'll never reach perfection until you're standing in Christ's presence. But you will experience more and more freedom in Christ as you surrender more and more of your life to His control.

The reason it's a process and not an instantaneous experience is because of sin. Old habits die hard. Selfishness is hard to give up. We're born with the propensity to think, "it's all about me." The sin of pride and self-sufficiency, in fact, is one of the most deeply rooted sins. To reach spiritual freedom, you must allow Christ to rule your life.

While Christ dealt with the penalty of sin on the cross, the process of freedom from slavery takes time. Romans 6:17–18 says, ".... though you used to be slaves to sin, you wholeheartedly obeyed the form of teaching to which you were entrusted. You have been set free from sin and have become slaves to righteousness." I know a man in his seventies who went to church for many years but never walked in spiritual freedom. Recently, I've watched this man take his spiritual growth seriously and make greater strides in spiritual victory than any previous steps. Before my very eyes, I saw a transformation taking place that really impressed me. This is what God wants to see in all of our lives. God is interested in transformation, and He accomplishes that transformation as we read the Word, pray, and relate to other believers in the body of Christ.

Try IT!

Mark those areas that are true. Liberty in Christ means:

☐ Change of mind, emotions, and as a consequence, a change of conduct.
☐ Freedom to do whatever comes naturally.
☐ Separation from areas of bondage brought on by sin and Satan.

You can start over anytime. You will sin and fail at various times on your Christian journey. This is to be expected. Yet, the Scripture says that when we sin, we have a way out. We can confess our sins to God. 1 John 1:9 declares, "If we confess our sins, he is faithful and just and will forgive us our sins and purify us from all unrighteousness." Some have appropriately referred to this verse as the Christian's "bar of soap." Whenever you realize you have made a mistake and have become "spiritually dirty" simply reach for the promised "bar of soap" and enjoy a free bath. Don't allow the enemy to condemn you to the point where you flee the fight. Keep your eyes on Jesus.

To confess means to see sin the same way that God sees it. It means to call sin a sin and to take personal responsibility for it, without making any excuse or blaming others.

Even though we are growing toward spiritual maturity, there's a part of each one of us that has a propensity to sin. We sin because we are sinners. Yet, in the process of becoming holy, God has given us the means of confessing our sins to Him and receiving forgiveness.

Psalm 51:4 declares, "Against You, You only, have I sinned and done what is evil in Your sight." God willingly receives us by His grace, but we do need to acknowledge that He's perfect and righteous and that our sins are against Him alone.

To experience spiritual freedom, we must decide to stop sinning and ask the Holy Spirit to make that a reality. We need to ask Him to help us overcome the temptation to sin. 1 Corinthians 10:13 says, "No temptation has seized you except what is common to man. And God is faithful; he will not let you be tempted beyond what you can bear. But when you are tempted, he will also provide a way out so that you can stand up under it."

Try IT!

Read 1 John 1:9.
What will God do if we confess our sins?

____

____

____

____

Are there sins in your life that you need to confess right now?

____

____

If so, confess them one by one and receive Christ's forgiveness.

____

____

____

____

____

____

____

____

Remember IT!

What verse did you read in this lesson that helped you the most?

____

____

____

____

____

____

____

Main points:

1. Scripture tells us what God thinks about us. We need to believe what God says and live the life He has planned for us.
2. Although Jesus has delivered us from the slavery of sin, we need to confess and renounce areas of sin and bondage in our lives, asking the Holy Spirit to control those areas and to give us spiritual freedom.

Apply IT!

1. Next time doubt arises in your mind about what God thinks of you, quote one of the meaningful verses you read in this lesson to counteract Satan's attempt to wound you.
2. Read your daily chapter with the view of discovering what God thinks about you.

Triumphing Over the Forces of Evil

During the Revolutionary War, it was easy for the Patriots to spot the English soldiers because they wore brightly colored uniforms. In guerilla warfare, however, it is much more difficult to spot the enemy. In the year 2000, while I was teaching a course in Bogota, Colombia, various students came up to me after class expressing fear for their safety. The terrorist guerillas who had infiltrated society looked just like everyone else. No one knew for sure if the police officer, clerk, or government official was a terrorist. Sometimes we are not aware of the enemy.

Christians are faced with three main enemies that often go undetected:

1. Satan and demonic forces.
2. The world—the system around us that is opposed to God (e.g., materialism, power, etc.).
3. The evil desires of our sinful nature (old self).

As you claim Christ's power over each of these invaders, you'll live a triumphant Christian life.

Satan and his demons

You don't need to fear Satan. Jesus defeated Satan on the cross; he is a defeated foe. 1 John 4:4 says, "You, dear children, are from God and have overcome them [false prophets], because the one who is in you is greater than the one who is in the world." John is saying here that God who is in you is much greater than the enemy (Satan) who is in the world. Because of who you are in Jesus and because the Spirit of God dwells in you, you don't need to fear Satan.

Having said that, you also need to realize that you are engaged in a spiritual battle and that Satan is alive and wants to deceive and destroy the people of God. Ephesians 6:12 says, "Put on the full armor of God so that you can take your stand against the devil's schemes. For our struggle is not against flesh and blood, but against the rulers, against the authorities, against the powers of this dark world and against the spiritual forces of evil in the heavenly realms."

Referring to Satan, Jesus said, "The thief comes only to steal and kill and destroy; I have come that they may have life, and have it to the full" (John 10:10).

Try IT!

Read James 4:7.
What are the two things that we must do to obtain victory over the devil?

___

___

___

In what areas in your own life do you need to resist the devil?

___

___

___

___

___

___

___

Inactivity is the worst possible option. Satan and his demons will take advantage of a lethargic attitude and conquer or retake areas of your life. Remember the exhortation in James 4:7: "Submit yourselves, then, to God. Resist the devil, and he will flee from you."
When I feel that demonic forces are attacking me, my family or others, I say, "Satan, I rebuke you [I name the area from which I'm rebuking Satan] in the name of Jesus Christ and by His powerful blood."

Do IT!
After determining areas in your life where Satan and his demons are attacking, confess any known sin and then resist the devil in the name of Jesus Christ and by the power of His shed blood.

The World

The word world conjures up images of planet earth seen from an orbiting satellite. The Bible, however, uses the term world to refer not only to the normal physical world around us, but also to a way of thinking that is contrary to God's will and under the control of Satan and sin. Often when the Bible uses the word world, it refers to Satan's rule and the kingdoms here on earth (remember that God is greater than Satan is and God ultimately controls all things).

Listen to how John describes this world in 1 John 5:19: "We know that we are children of God, and that the whole world is under the control of the evil one." It's obvious from this verse that world is used here to describe people's thinking and lifestyle opposed to God's plan. The devil persuades people to follow his plan because he controls the kingdoms of this world. One of the tricks Satan used in his attempt to cause Christ to stumble during the desert temptation was to offer worldly power. We read in Matthew 4:8–9 the devil took Jesus to a very high mountain and showed him all the kingdoms of the world and their splendor and then said, "All this I will give you," he said, "if you will bow down and worship me."

Jesus didn't give way to Satan's devices, but so many people do. Satan offers people riches and pleasures but enslaves them in the process. He'll try to do the same with you through pornography, lies, alcohol, etc.

Remember that it's not a sin to face temptation. A person should never feel guilty for being tempted. Temptation is simply the front door through which sin actually enters. Someone has said, "You can't stop the birds from flying over you, but you can prevent them from making nests on your head." In the same way, you can't prevent temptation from entering your life (Jesus Himself was tempted). You can, however, prevent temptation from dominating your life. When temptation comes, resist it, so it doesn't blossom into full-fledged sin. The good news is that God has promised to provide us a way out

Try IT!

Read 1 Corinthians 10:13.
What will God provide when we are tempted?

____

____

What temptations are you facing in your own life today?

____

____

What is God's "way out" for you?

____

____

____

____

____

The Sinful Nature

Most war stories have examples of enemy spies who were somehow able to penetrate the rank and file of the opposing army's high command. John Anthony Walker Jr., between 1967 and 1985, provided the KGB with vital U.S. cryptographic secrets that enabled Russian agents to decipher coded military messages. Soviet KGB General Boris Aleksandrovich Solomatin, who oversaw Walker, later called him the "most important" spy ever recruited by Russia.

One of the most subtle enemies of the believer lives within. Like an enemy spy, this enemy forms part of our nature. The Bible refers to this enemy as the sinful nature.

The Bible says that the sinful nature rebels against God and is in constant conflict with spiritual things.

Paul says in 2 Corinthians 5:17, "Therefore, if anyone is in Christ, he is a new creation; the old has gone, the new has come!" God gives us a new nature that is called a "new creation." This new creation or nature helps us to know God and understand spiritual things. God doesn't, however, take away our freedom of choice and our sinful nature. He allows the sinful nature to remain within us for the duration of our time on earth.

You've probably noticed the battle waging within and the tendency to rebel against God and His ways. The way to victory in the Christian life is to allow the Holy Spirit to control you. Galatians 5:16–17 sums it up beautifully, "So I say, live by the Spirit, and you will not gratify the desires of the sinful nature. For the sinful nature desires what is contrary to the Spirit, and the Spirit what is contrary to the sinful nature. They are in conflict with each other, so that you do not do what you want." The wise man Solomon has told us in Proverbs 3:5–6, "Trust in the LORD with all your heart and lean not on your own understanding; in all your ways acknowledge him, and he will make your paths straight."

Try IT!

Read Galatians 5:24-26
What does Paul tell us to do in order to live in the Spirit?

___

___

___

What are some things that you can do to live in the Spirit and avoid temptations?

___

___

___

___

___

___

___

___

___

We can be led by the Spirit and overcome our sinful nature by maintaining a vibrant Christian life. We do this by growing in an intimate relationship with God each day. This comes by reading God's Word, obeying what God says, and developing an intimate prayer relationship with Him (Ephesians 6:18; 1 Peter 2:2).

Claiming Victory in Christ

When the Roman army came back to Rome after conquering other nations, they would parade their defeated foes before the cheering throngs that lined the roads.

Christ's victory on the cross was more subtle. Everything indicated that Jesus had lost the battle. Just the opposite was true. Jesus overcame Satan on the cross. Colossians 2:15 says, "And having disarmed the powers and authorities, he made a public spectacle of them, triumphing over them by the cross." Jesus offers us victory over the devil, the world, and the sinful nature. He said in John 16:33, "In this world you will have trouble. But take heart! I have overcome the world."

Each believer must now apply Christ's victory, knowing that God has made us "more than conquerors." We can do this by maintaining an intimate relationship with God through prayer, reading the Word and walking in the Spirit.

In your daily walk with God, you'll find the wisdom and power to resist the devil.

Try IT!

Read 1 Corinthians 15:57.
What is the key to the victory in this verse?

____

____

____

____

____

Pray, "*God, I thank You that You have already paid the price for my victory by dying on the cross for my sins and rising again. As I battle with Satan, the world, and my own sinful nature, I claim your victory for me and my family.*"

Making Jesus the Lord of your life

During Christ's time on earth, he encountered many demon-possessed people. A legion of demons possessed one person in particular, and Jesus set him free. The change in this man was dramatic and Scripture describes him as "dressed and in his right mind" (Mk. 5:15). All this man wanted to do was follow Jesus because he was so completely transformed. When Jesus changes us, our desire is to follow Him and crown Him Lord of our lives.

Romans 10:9 says, "That if you confess with your mouth, "Jesus is Lord," and believe in your heart that God raised him from the dead, you will be saved." Jesus has the right to be Lord of your life because of who He is. He is the Lord of all creation, and the whole universe is subject to Him (see Colossians 1:16–18).

Try IT!

If you were to allow Jesus to rule as Lord in your life today, what would that mean practically for you?

____

____

____

____

____

____

____

____

____

____

He also should be Lord because of what He has done for you on the cross. He placed your sins on Himself and received God's judgment for you. He paid for all your sins with His blood. God should have condemned you because of your sin, but Jesus wiped away that judgment with His own blood. The Bible says, "you were bought at a price. Therefore honor God with your body" (1 Cor. 6:20).

Making Jesus Lord in practical terms means giving him control of your career, money, education, marriage, possessions, family, and leisure time. It's allowing Jesus to have His way in every area of your life.

Jesus, however, won't force you to make Him your Lord. We must be willing to make that decision in this life. In the next life, we won't have that choice. Romans 14:11–12 say, "For we will all stand before God's judgment seat. It is written: 'As surely as I live,' says the Lord, 'every knee will bow before me; every tongue will confess to God.' So then, each of us will give an account of himself to God."

Many centuries ago, Augustine was a wild young man who partied and slept with prostitutes. After he accepted Jesus Christ as Savior and Lord of his life, one of the prostitutes caught him by the arm and invited him to her room. He said, "I am sorry. The Augustine you know is dead. This is a new Augustine, and you do not know what sort of man he is." You will face similar situations. Just remember that the old you has been crucified with Christ and the new you is now risen with Christ and is a new creature. Live like one.

Memorize IT!

2 Corinthians 5:17: "Therefore, if anyone is in Christ, he is a new creation; the old has gone, the new has come!"

Remember IT!

What was the most important thing you learned in this lesson?

____

____

____

____

____

____

____

____

Main points:

1. The major enemies of the believer are the world, the sinful nature, and the devil.
2. We have victory over all three through the cross of Jesus Christ. We must, however, claim and live out that victory.
3. Making Jesus Christ Lord means surrendering every aspect of our lives and giving Him complete control.

Apply IT!

1. Confess and renounce any area of your life in which Satan, the world, or your sinful nature is controlling your life.
2. Ask Jesus to become Lord over every area of your life. Pray a prayer like this, *"Jesus, I give you control over ____________. I pray that you would fill me with your Spirit and give me the power and victory to overcome that particular aspect of my life."*

My Life and My Wallet

A farmer once called the office of the pastor asking to see "The Head Hog at the trough." The receptionist said, "Sir, if you're talking about our beloved Minster, you may call him Reverend or Pastor, but I don't think it would be proper to refer to him as 'The Head Hog at the trough.'" "Well, all right," the farmer said. "I just sold a few pigs and was going to donate ten thousand dollars to the building fund, so I was hoping to catch him." "Oh, just a minute, sir," the receptionist said, "I think I heard the little porker just come in!"

Money grabs people's attention.

Money is important. We need it to live and survive. And the Bible talks about it a lot! There are 40 verses on "baptism", 275 verses on "prayer", 350 verses on "faith", 650 verses on "love"— and 2,350 verses that specifically relate to finances and material possessions.

Making Jesus Lord of your life includes Lordship of your material possessions.

God's ownership

The Bible states that God is the owner of everything. He holds absolute rights over all of His creation because He made all things. He governs the entire universe and is worthy of the title Lord and Master. Palm 103:19 says, "The LORD has established his throne in heaven, and his kingdom rules over all."

But God is not only the sovereign ruler, He's also a loving and faithful provider that takes care of His creatures and meets their needs.

Try IT!

Read 1 Chronicles 29:11–12.
Where does wealth come from according to these verses?

____

____

____

Do you believe that God is the source of all wealth and prosperity in your life? Why or why not?

____

____

____

____

Even though everything belongs to God, He has delegated the administration of His creation to us. God calls us administrators or stewards of His creation. An administrator/steward knows he must give account of his stewardship (read 1 Corinthians 4:1–2). If a person is in a position of authority, it's because God has given him that particular administrative responsibility. The Bible says we are administrators of

- The earth. Genesis 1:28: tells us that we are to rule over the earth.
- The gifts of the Spirit. The Bible tells us in 1 Peter 4:10 that each of us has a spiritual gift and that we need to manage it well.
- The gospel message. 1 Corinthians 4:1–2 talks about being administrators of God's message that He's given to the church.

- Our physical possessions. 2 Corinthians 9:6–11 talks about sowing into the lives of others with the physical possessions that God has given to us.

Try IT!

Can you think of other things God wants us to care for?

____

____

____

____

____

____

We are His administrators

In 1980 I administrated my parent's apartment complex in downtown Long Beach. I had to collect rent, make repairs, and give general oversight. Ultimately, I had to submit to my Dad's direction because he owned the property.

God is the owner of this creation. All that we have comes directly from God: life, health, house, car, work, and money. Everything comes from Him and one day we will give an account to Him.

One person in the Bible named Job lost everything but said: "Naked I came from my mother's womb and naked I'll return. God has given and God has taken away. Blessed be God's name" (Job 1:21).

God has freely given us these things, and He can also take them away. In the meantime, He's given us the privilege of participating in administrating everything in His creation.

Try IT!

Of the things you have, what comes from God?

☐ Nothing
☐ Some things
☐ Everything

Our money belongs to God

Martin Luther once said, "People go through three conversions: their head, their heart and their pocketbook. Unfortunately, not all at the same time." When a person is ready to give part of their money to God, major value shifts have already taken place in their heart.

When the famous English preacher, John Wesley, visited his congregations, he would question his assistants about their progress in the faith. He would often ask if their Christianity had affected their pockets. Money is important, and God has permitted us to have it. Part of our responsibility to administrate money is to give back to God the portion that belongs to Him. The Bible talks about giving a tenth (tithe) of our income to God.

Memorize IT!

2 Corinthians 9:6: "Whoever sows sparingly will also reap sparingly, and whoever sows generously will also reap generously."

What is a tithe?

A tithe is the tenth part of what we earn that we set apart for God's use. We don't own that part—God does. We consecrate that tenth part to God for His glory. It doesn't belong to us; it belongs to Him.

The Bible talks about the tithe in various places. For example in Malachi 3:10 God says, "Bring the whole tithe into the storehouse, that there may be food in my house. Test me in this," says the LORD Almighty, "and see if I will not throw open the floodgates of heaven and pour out so much blessing that you will not have room enough for it."

There's actually a test linked to these verses. God asks us to test His faithfulness and willingness to pour out His Spirit upon us and bless everything we do. The test involves our giving to Him and allowing Him to give back to us. Of course, the idea of tithing was clearly highlighted in the Old Testament, but it's also something that Jesus talks about in Matthew 23:23. In this verse, Jesus tells the leaders of Israel not to neglect tithing but to focus, rather on justice, mercy and faithfulness.

We who have believed in Jesus and are under the grace of Christ are no longer obligated to keep the law. For those under the law, tithing was an obligation and if not obeyed, it resulted in a curse (Mal. 3:9). We should not give the tithe because of the fear of cursing, nor should we be motivated by the fact that if we give, He will give us much more.

Although there's a danger in over-emphasizing tithing (to the neglect of more important Biblical truth), there's also a danger of underemphasizing it, thus missing out on God's blessing. When my wife and I plan our budget, the first thing we do is to take our tithe and offerings out of what we gross. Not only do we want to obey God but we also want to receive His blessing. And we've tested God in this area over the years and have found Him one hundred percent faithful.

Do IT!

Don't miss God's blessing on your life. Determine right now to give ten percent of your income to God's work.

The Old Testament tithe was given to support God's priests and their ministry. In our time, we can direct our giving to primarily support God's work through the local church. Other places to give include missionary work, social outreach, and various Christ-honoring ministries.

Try IT!

Read 2 Corinthians 9:7
According to this verse, what should be our attitude when giving?

____

____

____

____

What has been your attitude in the past about giving?

____

____

____

____

____

____

____

____

Our motivation for giving

Our motivation for giving should be the free exercise of our love toward God because we are so grateful for what He has done for us. We should not give relucantly but generously from a thankful heart.

As you give, you'll receive so much more. In reality, you can't afford NOT to give generously. The assurance of God's blessing through sowing is something that God Himself promises. You and I need God's rich blessing that He promises when we give generously. God does not need to receive money from us. Tithing trains us to become givers like He is.

Two points about tithing deserve special attention. First, it's important to remember that tithing is a matter of priority. We think that we never have enough money for ourselves. We always want more. Tithing simply helps us to love God and His work more than things. Second, remember the promise of Malachi 3:10. God says, "Test me in this" This means that God wants us to test His faithfulness to provide for us after we've obeyed Him in this area.

You won't see the blessing of God until you decide to obey. It's necessary to trust God in this area in order to discover if He will keep His promise. It's a matter of faith.

Try IT!

Which of the following excuses have you used to forego giving?

- ☐ I don't have enough money.
- ☐ I have debts.
- ☐ I'm saving to buy a house, car, furniture, etc.
- ☐ I first need to fix my economic problems and then I'll begin to give.

God will provide in miraculous ways as you step out and give your tithes and offerings. You'll discover God doing wonderful things in your life. God will open the windows of heaven and give an abundant blessing in ways that you couldn't even imagine.

Remember IT!

What had the most impact for you in this lesson?

____

____

____

____

____

____

____

____

____

____

Main points:

1. God owns all things; we are administrators.
2. When we give our tithes and offerings, we glorify God and gain spiritual and physical rewards.
3. When we give in abundance, we reap in abundance.

Apply IT!

1. Pray and ask God to make you a faithful administrator of His possessions.
2. Commit yourself to give generously and watch God bless you abundantly.

Baptism and the Lord's Supper

The story is told about the baptism of King Aengus by St. Patrick in the middle of the fifth century. Sometime during the rite, St. Patrick leaned on his sharp-pointed staff and inadvertently stabbed the king's foot. After the baptism was over, St. Patrick looked down at all the blood, realized what he had done, and begged the king's forgiveness. Why did you suffer this pain in silence, St. Patrick wanted to know. The king replied, "I thought it was part of the ritual."

Baptism is attached to a particular ritual, but pain is not part of that ceremony. Jesus endured the pain on the cross and through faith in Him we have eternal life. Baptism is a symbolic practice that demonstrates our faith in Christ.

Baptism

Baptism is not necessary for you to become a Christian. The thief on the cross who died alongside Jesus wasn't baptized. He recognized that Jesus was suffering innocently while he himself was suffering for his misdeeds. He could only say to Jesus, "Remember me when you enter your kingdom." Jesus responded, "Today, you will be with me in paradise" (Luke 23:39–43). This man recognized that Jesus was the Savior of the world, wanted to be in His Kingdom, and called out to Him. The thief only had to believe to be saved.

If baptism doesn't save a person, then why should a person be baptized?

Two reasons for baptism

There are at least two main reasons why we should be baptized. The first reason is obedience. Jesus commanded His church "to make disciples of all nations, baptizing them in the name of the Father and of the Son and of the Holy Spirit" (Matthew 28:19). A disciple, according to Jesus, will be baptized.

The second reason is public identification with Christ. You need to be willing to unashamedly stand with Jesus in His death and resurrection. This is what baptism symbolizes. When a person enters the water, he is identifying with Christ in His death. When he comes out of the water, he is rising with Christ in His resurrection. Romans 6:3–4 says, "Or don't you know that all of us who were baptized into Christ Jesus were baptized into his death? We were therefore buried with him through baptism into death in order that, just as Christ was raised from the dead through the glory of the Father, we too may live a new life."

Try IT!

How do you feel when you think about being baptized?

____

____

____

____

____

____

I was saved during a revival period called the Jesus movement. Many longhaired hippies gave their lives to Jesus, and God used Chuck Smith to lead this growing movement. We continually heard stories of Pastor Chuck Smith baptizing many people in Southern California. Those baptized were so filled with the Holy Spirit that they spread the Jesus movement fire all over the country. In those days, following Jesus didn't seem like a complicated process.

Going down in the water means the end of the old self. You're committing yourself to live a new life in Christ (Romans 6:1–6). Baptism is a symbol and testimony of being dead to sin and the old way of living. When you come up from the water, it's a symbol of being identified with Christ in his resurrection. Identifying yourself with Christ through water baptism is a powerful way that you as a new believer can testify to your faith.

Try IT!

Mark true or false:

☐ Water baptism is an act of obedience.
☐ Water baptism is necessary for salvation.
☐ Water baptism is a public demonstration of a person's identification with Christ.
☐ Water baptism cleanses a person from sin.

Water baptism is an act of obedience through which believers publicly express their faith and commitment to Christ. It identifies a believer with Christ in His death and resurrection.

Examples of baptism in the Bible

Jesus Himself was baptized (submerged in water) in the River Jordan at the beginning of His ministry (Mt. 3:13–16).

The book of Acts is the history book of the early church. They took Christ's command literally. Right after the Holy Spirit descended in Acts chapter two, for example, Scripture says, "When the people heard this, they were cut to the heart and said to Peter and the other apostles, 'Brothers, what shall we do?' Peter replied, 'Repent and be baptized, every one of you, in the name of Jesus Christ for the forgiveness of your sins. And you will receive the gift of the Holy Spirit'" (2:37–38). The first response to the convicting work of the Holy Spirit was baptism.

Later in the book of Acts when the Holy Spirit used persecution to send His people to proclaim the gospel outside of Jerusalem, we read about Philip's ministry. Acts 8:12 says, "But when they believed Philip as he preached the good news of the kingdom of God and the name of Jesus Christ, they were baptized, both men and women."

Try IT!

Read Acts 8:35–38.
What did Phillip announce to this man?

____

____

____

What was the requirement of this man in order to be baptized?

____

____

____

Many more Biblical examples show the same pattern. The order is similar throughout the Bible:

1. The good news about Jesus was announced.
2. Those who heard believed in Jesus.
3. They were baptized.

Baptism identified Christ's followers then and today. When you are baptized, you'll also notice that you place a stake in the ground that serves as a reference point for your faith. You can look back to your baptism as the moment when you publicly declared your faith in Christ. This reference point will remind you that you obeyed God's Word to openly identify with Jesus in His death and resurrection.

Do IT!

Plan now to be baptized in water. Talk to your cell leader, coach, or pastor about your desire to obey the command of Christ to be baptized.

The Lord's Supper

A Methodist dentist, Dr. Thomas Welch, objected to his church's use of fermented wine in the communion service. Experimenting at night in his kitchen, he came up with a nonalcoholic grape beverage, which he named "Dr. Welch's Unfermented Wine". He approached church officials to persuade them to substitute his beverage for the traditional wine. The elders regarded his suggestion as an unacceptable innovation. His son, Charles, who was also a dentist, changed the name to Welch's Grape Juice, and found so much demand he went into fulltime business selling Welch's grape juice.

Many churches use Welch's grape juice to symbolize Christ's blood. But whether a church uses Welch's grape juice, real wine, bread, or crackers, the person behind the elements is what the Lord's Supper is really about.

The Lord's Supper celebrates Christ's death. The Lord's Supper is an object lesson that represents a great spiritual truth for believers. The spiritual lesson is that Jesus died for our sins and is coming again soon.

The Lord's Supper reminds us of Christ's death

1 Corinthians 11:23–24 says, "The Lord Jesus, on the night He was betrayed, took bread … .and when He had given thanks, He broke it and said, 'This is my body, which is for you; eat it in remembrance of me.'"

When we participate in the ceremony called the Lord's Supper, we're remembering that Jesus died on the cross for our sins. We celebrate the Lord's Supper to remember what Jesus did for us on the cross. Jesus Himself instituted the Lord's Supper. The wine is red in color and represents the blood of Jesus that was shed on the cross for our sins. When we pass around cup and bread, we are not literally eating the body and blood of Christ. We are simply remembering what he did for us.

In 1 Corinthians 11:25, the Bible says, "In the same way, He took the cup, saying, 'This cup is the new covenant in my blood; drink it to remember me.'" The cup is a symbol of Christ's blood sacrifice shed for you and for me. When we participate in communion in the cell group or in the large group service, we reflect back on what Jesus has done for us on the cross—His crucified body and shed blood free us from our sin. The cup and the bread are symbols of what Jesus did on the cross for us. Christ commanded us to remember his death and resurrection through these symbols.

Try IT!

Read Luke 22:17–20.
Describe how Jesus must have felt since he knew this would be the Last Supper with His disciples

___

___

___

Why do you think it's important to participate in the Lord's Supper?

___

___

___

___

___

The Lord's Supper reminds us that Jesus is coming again

As we participate in the Lord's Supper we're reminded that Jesus Christ is coming soon. 1 Corinthians 11:26 says, "For whenever you eat the bread and drink the cup, you proclaim the Lord's death until He comes back." Until Jesus Christ comes back we are called to celebrate the Lord's Supper in appreciation for what He has already done for us and the anticipation of the glorious future that awaits us.

Who should take the Lord's Supper?

Jesus died for the sins of the entire world. He loves everyone. The Lord's Supper, however, is a time for serious reflection on what Jesus has accomplished on the cross. Since only believers can seriously reflect on Christ's death and resurrection in a personal, meaningful way, the Lord's Supper is for those who have a personal relationship with Jesus Christ. Paul the apostle rebukes some in his day who were more concerned about partying than reflecting on Jesus: "For anyone who eats and drinks without recognizing the body of the Lord eats and drinks judgment upon himself" (1 Cor. 11:29).

Before sharing in the Lord's Supper, it's important to spend some time in self-examination and reflection on what Jesus had done. Remember what the Psalmist said, "If I had cherished sin in my heart, the Lord would not have listened" (Psalm 66:18). I try to confess any known sin in my own life (e.g., bitterness, anger, etc.) and prepare my heart to partake in the Lord's Supper. Take time to think of Christ's incredible sacrifice and the freedom He now offers.

Even though people who share in the Lord's Supper should be followers of Jesus, we must remember that all of us are in the process of maturity and we should resist the condemnation of trying to be perfect before sharing in the Lord's Supper.

Memorize IT!

1 Corinthians 11:25: "In the same way, after supper he [Jesus] took the cup, saying, "This cup is the new covenant in my blood; do this, whenever you drink it, in remembrance of me."

When and how often should we observe the Lord's Supper?

The Lord's Supper can take place as often as believers get together. It is not a ritual, so there is no defined time to observe it. Some cell churches take the Lord's Supper in the cell group while others take it in the celebration service. I would recommend a combination approach. At times, it's great to celebrate the Lord's Supper with everyone present but it's also very special to celebrate it in the intimate atmosphere of the home.

Try IT!

Mark true or false:

☐ The Lord's Supper is for believers.
☐ The Lord's Supper is for unbelievers.
☐ The Lord's Supper is symbolic of Christ's death and resurrection.

Remember IT!

What had the most impact for you in this lesson? ____________

____

____

____

____

____

____

____

Main points:

1. Baptism is a command that must be obeyed by all those who are Christ's disciples.
2. Baptism is a public testimony to something that already occurred when you received Jesus as Savior and Lord.
3. The Lord's Supper helps us to remember Christ's death until He comes again.

Apply IT!

1. Talk to your cell leader or pastor about baptism.
2. Get baptized.
3. Participate in the Lord's Supper in the cell or in the celebration.

How to Coach Someone Using this Material

Many churches will teach this material in a group setting. This is the normal way to use the material, but it's not the only way. If you choose to teach a group of people, outlines and PowerPoints are provided for all five equipping books on a CD. Purchase this CD at www.joelcomiskeygroup.com or by calling 1-888-344-CELL.

Another way to train someone is to allow the person to complete each lesson individually and then ask someone of the same gender to coach him or her. The coach would hold the "trainee" responsible to complete the lesson and share what he or she is learning.

I believe in multiple methods for teaching material. The fact is that not everyone can attend group-training meetings. But the person still needs training. Coaching is a great option.

Coaching the trainee through the material

Ideally, the coach will meet with the trainee after each lesson. At times, however, the trainee will complete more than one lesson and the coach will combine those lessons when they meet together.

The coach is a person who has already gone through the material and is now helping someone else in the training process. Additionally a coach must have:

- a close walk with Jesus.
- a willing, helpful spirit. The coach doesn't need to be a "teacher." The book itself is the teacher—the coach simply holds the trainee accountable with asking questions and prayerful encouragement.

I recommend my book, *How to be a Great Cell Group Coach*, for additional understanding of the coaching process (this book can also be purchased on the JCG web site or by calling 1-888-344 CELL). The principles in *How to be a Great Cell Group Coach* apply not only to coaching cell leaders but also to coaching a trainee. I recommend the following principles:

- Receive from God. The coach must receive illumination from Jesus through prayer so he has something of value to give to the trainee.
- Listen to the person. The coach's job is to listen to the trainee's answers. The coach should also listen to the trainee's joys, struggles, and prayer concerns.
- Encourage the trainee. Often the best thing the coach can do is point out areas of strength. I tell coaches to be a fanatic for encouragement. We all know our failures and have far too much condemnation hanging over us. Encouragement will help the trainee press on and look forward to each lesson. Try to start each lesson by pointing out something positive about the person or about what he or she is doing.
- Care for the person. The person might be struggling with something above and beyond the lesson. The material might bring out that specific problematic area. The best coaches are willing to touch those areas of deep need through prayer and counsel. And it's one hundred percent acceptable for the coach to simply say, "I don't have an answer for your dilemma right now, but I know someone who does." The coach can then go to his or her own coach to find the answer and bring it back the next week.
- Develop/train the person. Hopefully the person has already read the lesson. The goal of the coach is to facilitate the learning process by asking specific questions about the lesson.
- Strategize with the trainee. The coach's job is to hold the trainee accountable to complete the next lesson and/or finish the current one. The coach's main role is to help the trainee sustain the pace and get the most out of the material.
- Challenge the person. Some think that caring is good but confronting is wrong. The word care-fronting combines the two

and is what the Bible promotes. If we truly care, we'll confront. The Spirit might show you areas in the trainee's life that need to come under the Lordship of Christ. The best approach is to ask for permission. You might say, "Tom, may I have permission to speak to you about something I'm noticing?" After the person gives you permission, you can then tell him what the Lord is laying on your heart.

First session

When the coach meets with the trainee, the Holy Spirit will guide the session. Creativity and flexibility should reign. I do recommend, however, the following principles:

- Get to know the person. A great way to start is to use the Quaker questions. This will help you to warm up to each other. After the first week, the coach can open in prayer and simply ask about the trainee's life (e.g., family, work, studies, spiritual growth, etc.)

Quaker questions

1. Where did you live between the ages of 7–12?
2. How many brothers and sisters did you have?
3. What form of transportation did your family use?
4. Whom did you feel closest to during those years?

- Be transparent. Since you've already completed this training material, share your experiences with the trainee. Transparency goes a long way. Great coaches share both victories and struggles.

"Coaching questions" to use each week

A great coach asks lots of questions and listens intently. The goal is to draw the answers from the trainee so that he or she applies the material to daily living. Key questions to ask each time are:

1. What did you like best about the lesson(s)?
2. What did you like least about the lesson(s)?
3. What did you not understand?

4. What did you learn about God that you didn't know previously?
5. What do you personally need to do about it?

The coach doesn't have to ask each of the above questions, but it is good to get into a pattern, so the trainee knows what to expect each week.

Pattern to follow each week

1. Prepare yourself spiritually before the session begins.
2. Read the lesson in advance, remembering the thoughts and questions you had when you went through the material.
3. Start the session in prayer.
4. Ask the coaching questions.
5. Trust the Holy Spirit to mold and shape the trainee.
6. Close in prayer.

Index

A

Abba,27
Acts,9, 14, 36, 37, 39, 73, 74
administrators,64, 65, 70
apostle,9, 36, 37, 77
Augustine,61

B

Baptism,3, 71, 73, 74, 78, 71
Bible,2, 5, 9, 8, 10, 11, 12, 13, 14, 17, 19, 20, 21, 20, 21, 22, 23, 24, 25, 26, 31, 32, 40, 43, 45, 46, 55, 57, 61, 63, 64, 65, 66, 73, 74, 75, 79, 81
Billy Graham,11, 41
blood,54, 71, 75, 76, 55, 61, 77

C

cell-based church,37
cell church,37, 40
cell group,37, 38, 39, 42, 75, 77
cell group coach,9, 36, 37, 77
Christ,1, 2, 5, 8, 9, 8, 9, 10, 11, 12, 14, 15, 18, 21, 24, 32, 34, 35, 36, 39, 40, 41, 43, 45, 49, 44, 46, 44, 29, 27, 45, 46, 47, 48, 49, 50, 51, 53, 55, 57, 59, 60, 61, 62, 67, 71, 72, 73, 74, 75, 76, 77, 78, 81
Chuck Smith,72
church,11, 19, 21, 23, 33, 35, 36, 37, 38, 39, 40, 41, 42, 49, 64, 67, 71, 73, 75
commandment,24
Corinthians,11, 35, 44, 47, 56, 57, 59, 64, 65, 45, 50, 68, 75, 76, 77
cross,5, 11, 49, 59, 62, 71, 75, 76, 77, 14, 53, 59, 61

D

death,9, 8, 11, 14, 24, 72, 73, 74, 75, 76, 77, 78
demons,53, 55, 60
devil,54, 59, 62, 54, 55

E

Emancipation Proclamation,46
encouragement,80
Ephesians,12, 31, 40, 43, 45, 48, 58, 41, 45, 54
eternal life,8, 9, 11, 12, 14, 15, 71

F

false prophets,, 53
Father,5, 8, 11, 14, 24, 44, 72, 27, 28, 29, 34, 36, 45
fear,10, 32, 38
fellowship,15
forgiveness,11, 14, 50, 51, 71, 73

G

gift,8, 9, 12, 13, 14, 64, 73
gospel,11, 14, 15, 64, 73
grace,12, 13, 31, 44, 47, 50, 67
Greek,22, 23, 35

H

Hebrews,36, 39, 42
hell,9
holiness,8
Holy Spirit,5, 14, 15, 17, 18, 20, 17, 20, 23, 24, 27, 42, 43, 45, 50, 52, 57, 72, 73, 81, 82

I

inspiration,19

J

Jesus,3, 5, 8, 8, 9, 10, 11, 12, 13, 18, 21, 24, 25, 29, 32, 33, 27, 15, 55, 46, 35, 33, 17, 14, 34, 39, 27, 34, 35, 36, 39, 41, 44, 45, 46, 47, 50, 52, 53, 54, 55, 56, 59, 60, 61, 62, 63, 67, 71, 72, 73, 74, 75, 76, 77, 78, 79, 80
Jew,36, 39
Job,65
John Wesley,66
justified,12, 13

L

Lordship,36, 63, 81

M

Malachi,66, 69
Martin Luther,66
Matthew,17, 18, 24, 29, 34, 47, 55, 67, 72
Michelangelo,49

N

New International Version,2, 22, 23
New Testament,15, 19, 21, 22, 23, 35

O

obedience,23
Old Testament,19, 21, 22, 39, 67

P

Philemon,21
Philippians,44, 46
pray,14, 26, 29, 30, 31, 32, 33, 34, 50, 62
prayer,29, 30, 32, 34

R

relationship,5, 9, 9, 11, 12, 14, 21, 27, 27, 28, 29, 30, 31, 38, 39, 41, 58, 59, 77
resurrection,9, 14, 24, 35, 72, 73, 74, 76, 77, 78
Revolutionary War,, 53
righteousness,9, 19, 44, 49
Romans,8, 12, 13, 27, 43, 44, 49, 60, 61, 72, 73

S

Salvation,12
Satan,50, 52, 59, 62, 53, 54, 59, 55
Scriptures,11, 39
separation,8
servant,27, 45
sin,8, 9, 11, 23, 31, 33, 44, 46, 49, 50, 52, 55, 56, 61, 73, 76, 77
spiritual,15, 18, 38, 39, 49, 50, 82
St. Patrick,71
steward,64
symbol,75

T

temptation,56
Timothy,19
Titanic,8, 32
tithing,69
transformation,49, 50
translations,22, 23

U

unforgiveness,47

V

victory,3, 43, 59

W

world,10, 11, 45, 21, 39, 53, 54, 46, 55, 59, 62, 71, 77

CPSIA information can be obtained
at www.ICGtesting.com
Printed in the USA
FFOW05n0355220515